Rise2Boss

From Employee to
Successfully Unemployed

JAMES BECTON

Foreword

Rise2Boss is a toolbox filled with the wisdom you need to become a true BOSS. It's not just about what you do—it's all about who you're becoming. Immerse yourself in this book, put its teachings into action, and get ready to shape-shift into the ultimate BOSS. Get ready to craft your dream business and live a life that's a dream come true.

This book is dedicated to all the dreamers who believe in the extraordinary power of entrepreneurship. Your perseverance, passion, and relentless pursuit of greatness have inspired me beyond words. As you begin this life-transforming journey, may you draw strength from the profound reservoirs of courage and resilience within you.

To my fellow dreamers and visionaries who have yearned for something more in their professional lives, may this book serve as a guiding light, illuminating the path to self-discovery and empowerment. I hope these pages resonate with you, fueling your belief in your inherent boundless potential.

For those aspiring entrepreneurs who stand on the precipice, ready to leap into the unknown, I commend your bravery and embrace your willingness to transcend the confines of comfort. Remember, within every challenge lies an opportunity for growth, and within every setback lies the potential for a powerful comeback and a chance to learn from your mistakes.

I extend my deepest appreciation to the support networks of these aspiring entrepreneurs—families, friends, mentors, and colleagues. Your unwavering belief, encouragement, and understanding have nurtured their dreams and ambitions. You are the pillars of strength that uplift these astonishing dreamers on their exhilarating path.

And to all of you, my dear readers, who are embarking on this transformation, I thank you for joining me on this journey of self-discovery. Your trust in my words and willingness to embrace change fills my heart with immense gratitude. It is through your journey that I find purpose in my professional life.

May this book become the catalyst for your growth, a boundless source of motivation, and a reminder that the power to create a purposeful life filled with passion and success resides within you. As you turn these pages, may you unleash your inner boss and forge a fire that kindles the flame of greatness.

Together, we shall unveil the secrets of transitioning from an employee to an entrepreneur—the "Rise2Boss," as I like to call it. The path may be challenging, but you can conquer any obstacles with unwavering determination and the right mindset.

Let's discover your potential, embrace change, and craft a life of fulfillment and success beyond your wildest dreams. Let's step boldly into the unknown and unlock the door to limitless possibilities.

With boundless gratitude and unwavering determination,

James Becton

TABLE OF CONTENTS

Defining Rise2Boss

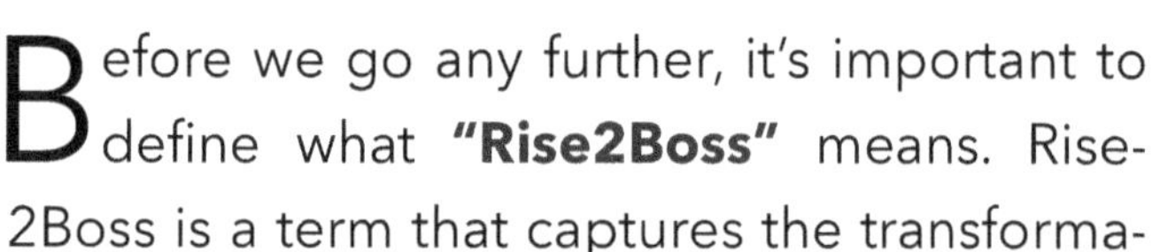

Before we go any further, it's important to define what **"Rise2Boss"** means. Rise-2Boss is a term that captures the transformative journey from a 9-to-5 job to the autonomy of becoming an entrepreneur who is the master of their own destiny.

Rise: This signifies the transition from the ordinary to the extraordinary. It's not just about leaving a regular job but about elevating oneself to a higher level of personal and professional achievement. Instead of climbing the corporate ladder, it's about ascending your own ladder, each rung moving you closer to your goals and potential.

BOSS: Becoming a Business Optimization Success Strategist (BOSS) means that you embody leadership, autonomy, and control. Becoming a BOSS signifies a monumental shift in professional identity. No longer an employee, you become a visionary steering your own ship. A BOSS specializes in maximizing business performance for success. They streamline operations, boost efficiency, and make strategic decisions that elevate productivity and profitability. Their vision extends beyond financial metrics; it encompasses personal growth, job satisfaction, and broader community influence.

A BOSS crafts strategies that cover all entrepreneurship facets, from identifying growth avenues to tackling challenges. They mentor those transitioning from traditional roles to entrepreneurship, ensuring they capitalize on their innate skills and passions. At their core, a BOSS is a problem-solver and leader, driving both financial and social impact while guiding teams toward success.

Rise2Boss: This melds the above concepts into a narrative of empowerment. It represents the transformative journey from a routine-driven life to one shaped by passion and purpose. Simply put, **"Rise2Boss"** illustrates the evolution from being an employee to a visionary leader, marking the shift from mere existence to thriving and making a lasting impact on the world.

Introduction

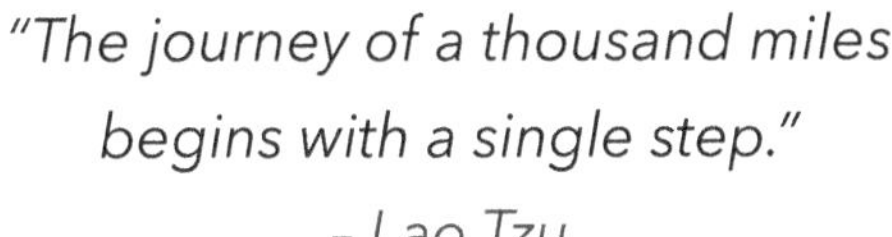

"The journey of a thousand miles begins with a single step."
- Lao Tzu

Congratulations on starting your incredible journey of self-discovery and transformation with *Rise2Boss: How to Become Successfully Unemployed*. This isn't just a book—it's a gateway to a new chapter in your life. Within these pages, you'll uncover the secrets that propelled me from a corporate cog to a visionary entrepreneur, guided by the invaluable insights of my mentor, the legendary Myron Golden.

It was while working with Myron that I discovered the four cornerstones of business growth: lead generation, lead conversion, customer ascension, and customer retention.

These principles were my compass as I navigated the uncharted waters of entrepreneurship, mastering the art of networking, communication, and strategic decision-making.

However, it's important for you to see that my journey wasn't just about triumphs. I also had to conquer the realities many entrepreneurs face. My journey is a testament to personal growth, resilience, and finding the balance between my work and personal relationships. Throughout it all, I've learned that success transcends financial achievements—it's about the lives we touch and the legacies we craft.

I've always sought to transcend the boundaries of my managerial role in the vast landscape of my corporate endeavors. Everything I did to move from an employee to a BOSS is reflected in the structure of this book, and my journey is a testament to my pursuit of a life beyond the confines of the conventional.

Therefore, this book encapsulates the essence of being a BOSS, and is divided into four key Parts: Transformation, Strategies,

Success, and Impact. Each of these Parts represents a different facet of being a BOSS.

In **Part I: Transformation**, you'll be guided from the monotony of daily jobs to the exhilarating world of entrepreneurship, taking control and steering your destiny with passion and purpose.

In **Part II: Strategies**, I will reveal important strategies that will guide your success as a BOSS. You will learn how to embrace strategic planning, navigate challenges effectively, and harness your creativity.

In **Part III: Success**, we will uncover that success is defined not only by achievements but by identifying and mastering your unique skills, converging your passion and expertise. I will additionally reveal the four pivotal moves for business growth: lead generation, lead conversion, customer ascension, and retention.

Finally, **Part IV: Impact** emphasizes that beyond the profit-driven nature of business, being a true BOSS means leveraging your entrepreneurial prowess to craft solutions that significantly enhance people's lives, creating a lasting impact on the world.

My Story

As a Manager, I thrived, taking on challenges with a fervor that set me apart in the corporate realm. Projects at Miller-Coors that yielded significant savings and collaborations bridging giants like General Motors and Amazon were not just tasks; they were my canvas for innovation. However, despite these monumental achievements, true recognition and reward often seemed just out of reach.

While management was fulfilling, it eventually became less a challenge and more a repetitive routine. The Profit and Loss responsibilities that once invigorated me now felt limiting. The weight of the mundane grew heavy, and I found myself yearning for more—a transformation from a Manager to a true CEO.

Years passed, and the feeling of entrapment persisted. I was underutilized, my potential untapped, my aspirations deferred. My vision for my life and family remained locked in the recesses of my mind, dormant and unfulfilled.

But one day, I made a decision that would forever alter my course.

While still managing for General Motors, I embarked on a journey to create my own trucking business. The leap was daring, as I had never driven a semi-truck before. However, the essence of business management was etched into my DNA, and success followed.

Yet, the world of trucking, while profitable, was not my true calling. Every day felt like labor, and the passion I sought evaded me. Then, as COVID-19 swept across the globe and casted a shadow of uncertainty, I found clarity. I reflected on my true passions and pondered how I could manifest them into a business. From this introspection, my new venture was born—a Business Optimization Success Strategist, or BOSS for short.

A BOSS is a visionary leader who optimizes business performance, extends their influence beyond financial metrics, and mentors aspiring entrepreneurs, emphasizing both financial and social impact. I aspired to empower fellow business owners who, like me, grappled with the tumultuous seas of entrepreneurship, especially during times like the pandemic. This vision emerged from the challenges faced by my trucking company, which nearly collapsed due to limited resources. This experience ignited our mission: to educate small business owners about the intricate world of genuine business credit and the art of becoming fundable.

Being a BOSS represents the resilience, passion, and unwavering commitment displayed by those bold enough to leap into entrepreneurship. It's about more than just financial liberation; it's about empowering business owners to seize control of their destiny.

My aspiration was clear—to provide a service capable of producing a profound impact on business owners, freeing them from the shackles of financial entanglement with their businesses. It was a mission to secure not only their financial well-being but also the prosperity of their families.

In the pages that follow, you will embark on a journey that transcends the traditional bounds of employment. It's a journey of transformation, self-discovery, and triumph—a journey from employee to entrepreneur. My hope is that my story will inspire all those who dare to dream, all those who yearn for something more, to take that leap of faith and rise to become the true bosses of their own destinies.

Rise2Boss is more than my story. It's a roadmap for anyone seeking to transition from employee to entrepreneur. Let my experiences inspire you, fuel your passion, and guide you in crafting your own success story.

Your adventure begins now.

Part I:

Transformation

In Part I we will begin by laying the foundational mindset and self-awareness crucial to becoming a BOSS.

Picture yourself soaring upward on a journey that bids farewell to the mundane routine of jobs, propelling you headfirst into entrepreneurship. We're talking about a monumental change: trading in your monotonous clock-watching existence for a life dictated by passion and purpose, breaking free from the shackles of limits and bursting through the frontiers of possibility. It's time to **transform** from being just another worker bee to taking charge of your own destiny to become a true BOSS.

In Part I, you will:

1) **Recognize the Internal Call:** Understand the deep-seated feelings of "longing for more" and how they signal a pull toward entrepreneurship.

2) **Navigate Fears and Doubts:** Develop strategies to confront uncertainties and view them as opportunities rather than barriers.

3) **Master Mind Hacking:** Acquire tools and techniques to optimize and re-shape your mindset, turning it into a powerful ally.

4) **Understand Self-Realization:** Follow a 5-step roadmap to harness your true potential, leading you from Zones of Competence to your unique Zone of Genius.

5) **Identify and Leverage Strengths:** Gain insights into the importance of self-awareness and how to strategically use your innate strengths in your entrepreneurial journey.

1.1
Longing for More

"The future depends on what you do today."
– Mahatma Gandhi

While working as a dedicated Process Improvement Specialist, I yearned for more. Each morning, it felt as though the wind was whispering to me of unexplored horizons, urging me to fulfill my potential. Then, one morning, it came to me. I was sipping my morning coffee and watching the sun rise over the bustling city when I felt it. A wave of potential. The feeling, the *longing*, was undeniable—it was a call to embrace entrepreneurship.

This internal pull wasn't to be ignored. It was a call to action, a beacon toward growth and fulfillment. So, rather than brushing it aside or ignoring it, I leaned in.

Overcoming Fear and Doubt

Yet, this journey would not be without its shadows. Every transition comes with its uncertainties, and the journey to entrepreneurship is no exception. However, it's important to remember that these fears and doubts aren't barriers—they're opportunities. We must face our fears head-on if we are to grow, and we must be determined to continually adjust our approaches in the face of failure.

Your mindset is critical to facing fear, doubt, and failure, which we will learn in more detail in section 1.2. You must refuse to succumb to fear and learn that it is not a roadblock but a steppingstone toward your true potential.

Discovering Your True Calling

This journey of embracing challenges and navigating uncertainties led to a profound self-discovery. Success is not predetermined—it is crafted. Becoming an entrepreneur is about aligning passion with purpose, breaking free from conventions, and daring to venture beyond the familiar. It's about recognizing our potential, exploring new avenues, and having the courage to redefine our path.

In this transformative phase, driven by my deep-seated desire to make a change, I ventured into new territories. I knew that I was capable of more than my day job, and the desire to create, innovate, and lead burned within me. I yearned to build something meaningful and be the architect of my destiny. As you're reading this book, I'm sure this is a feeling that you can relate to. This is why when the unknown beckons, you must be ready to answer its call.

As you embark on your entrepreneurial journey, it's essential to recognize that success isn't determined by external factors alone.

Although your mind holds endless possibilities, if not used effectively, it can become your greatest hurdle. It's crucial to navigate and master your mind to harness the opportunities around you. Your external achievements will often mirror how well you can hack your mind.

1.2
Practicing Mind Hacking

"Whether you think you can, or you think you can't – you're right."
– Henry Ford

"Mind hacking" is the ability to effectively understand, navigate, and optimize the intricate pathways of your mind. To succeed as a BOSS, I learned that you must be able to recognize and challenge limiting beliefs, reshape regressive thoughts, and adopt techniques and tools that foster a growth-oriented mindset.

Mind hacking will empower you to reframe challenges into opportunities, replace fears with excitement for growth, and channel your energy into achieving your goals.

Mastering Your Mind

Just as a hacker navigates the digital landscape, you can traverse and optimize the intricate pathways of your mind. During my entrepreneurship journey, I discovered that my thoughts were like lines of code that could be optimized for performance. This self-actualization empowered me to recognize and challenge the limiting beliefs that had quietly taken root over the years.

Therefore, I worked to identify the beliefs that whispered uncertainties to me and confronted them head-on. I dissolved my paralyzing belief that I was incapable of success and my persistent fear of failure. It's likely that you are experiencing similar fears, which is why I want to offer you the toolkit to rewrite your mental script.

Harnessing the Mind Hacker's Toolkit

The mind hacker's toolkit is a treasure trove of techniques that will rewire your neural pathways and pave the way for a growth-oriented mindset. You can find this toolkit below:

- **Cultivate a Growth Mindset**
  - Understand that thoughts are malleable and can be influenced.
  - View failure not as a dead end but as a learning opportunity on your path to success.
  - Recognize that with each belief you overcome, you free yourself from past constraints and empower your future.

- **Adopt Powerful Techniques**
  - Use positive affirmations to transition from negative self-talk to empowering narratives.
  - Conduct visualization exercises to clearly envision your goals and the steps to achieve them.
  - Practice mindfulness to stay anchored in the present, free from past regrets and future anxieties.

- Embrace gratitude to focus on the abundance in your life, fostering positivity and resilience.

- **Unleash Your Inner BOSS**

  - Reprogram your thoughts and beliefs to align with your goals and aspirations.

  - Replace fear of failure with excitement for growth and learning.

  - Recognize the power within you to drive your journey forward, embodying confidence and determination.

  - Understand that by mastering your mind, you're not just a passive observer but the active conductor of your success story.

If you follow this toolkit, you will no longer be a bystander to your own mind. Instead, you will be the conductor of your own reality. Through mind hacking, I transformed my mindset and was better able to embrace the challenges and triumphs that lay ahead on my entrepreneurial journey. If you follow the advice above, you will be well on your way to doing the same.

1.3
Understanding Self-Realization

"Every man has his own vocation;
talent is the call."
– Ralph Waldo Emerson

Once you gain mastery over your mind, the stage will be set for your next step: identifying and optimizing your unique strengths and passions. Guided by the timeless wisdom of Ralph Waldo Emerson, we will now explore the five-step roadmap to harnessing our true potential, ensuring that our entrepreneurial journeys resonate with our passions.

1) Identifying Your Zones of Incompetence and Competence

To truly harness your potential, it's essential to understand the zones that define your abilities. The Zones of Incompetence and Competence represent areas where you might struggle or perform adequately but without genuine passion. Recognizing these zones allows you to delegate or outsource tasks that don't align with your strengths. By focusing on what you excel at, you can invest your time and energy more effectively into endeavors that align more closely with your aspirations.

2) Reaching Your Zone of Excellence

Everyone has a realm where they excel and achieve commendable results. I call this the Zone of Excellence; it holds value and recognition. However, while it's rewarding to operate in this zone, it's crucial not to linger here for too long. True fulfillment often lies beyond this zone, in areas that challenge and excite you even more. Aim higher and seek out the next zone—the elusive Zone of Genius.

3) Optimizing Your Zone of Genius

Your Zone of Genius is where your innate talents and passions converge. For many—including myself—this zone is where they feel most alive. It is a place where you can create, innovate, and impact the world with unwavering enthusiasm. For instance, if sales and marketing resonate deeply with you, that might be where your genius lies. The key is to discover this zone, refine your skills within it, and let it guide your entrepreneurial journey.

4) From Passion to Expertise

Once you've identified your passion, the next step is to transform it into expertise. Dive deep into learning and continuously refine your skills. This dedication will elevate your capabilities, setting you apart from the rest.

5) Building a Business Around Your Genius

Armed with a clear understanding of your Zone of Genius, you're poised to build a business that truly reflects it. Let every strategy, decision, and action be informed by this entrenched passion and expertise. This alignment not only ensures success but also brings authenticity and purpose to your endeavors.

By understanding and navigating these zones—from competence to genius—you position yourself at the forefront of authentic success. As you move forward, remember that the foundation of any thriving business is not just in its strategy or resources but in the genuine passion and expertise of its founder. Embrace your unique strengths, continuously refine your skills, and let your Zone of Genius guide you on your journey.

1.4
Comprehending Strengths

"Knowing yourself is the beginning of all wisdom."
- Aristotle

Now that you can navigate your mind and identify your Zones of Competence and genius, we will move on to recognizing your unique strengths. The wisdom of both Emerson and Aristotle converse on this point: self-awareness is the foundation of all growth and achievement. Therefore, we will explore the importance of comprehending and leveraging your strengths to access your untapped potential.

During my own journey, I discovered that strengths aren't just abstract concepts; they're tangible assets that can drive significant impact. For instance, my natural inclination for problem-solving and critical thinking allows me to navigate complex situations, identify hidden patterns, and devise innovative solutions. Such skills are invaluable in the unpredictable landscape of entrepreneurship, where clarity and confidence are paramount.

Another revelation was the power of effective communication and interpersonal skills. Building genuine connections, fostering relationships, and inspiring those around you can be transformative in business. These skills not only facilitate networking but also help in building lasting partnerships and motivating teams. When I realized my natural inclination for communication, I leveraged it to assist me in reaching success.

To comprehend your own strengths, I recommend the following:

- **Self-Reflection and Awareness:** Understanding your strengths requires introspection and self-awareness. Reflecting on past experiences, challenges, and triumphs can provide insights into your unique skill set, forming a narrative that defines your entrepreneurial identity.

- **Harnessing Your Strengths:** Once identified, it's essential to actively nurture and refine these strengths. For example, if problem-solving is a standout skill, make it a focal point in your entrepreneurial endeavors, letting it guide your decisions and strategies.

- **Surround Yourself with Complementary Skills:** No one is a master of all trades. With this insight, it's wise to surround yourself with a team whose strengths fill in your gaps. By doing so, you ensure a holistic approach to your venture and gain a team that blends diverse skills.

Think of your entrepreneurial journey as a symphony. Just as an orchestra brings together various instruments to produce a masterpiece, your strengths, skills, and the team you build will come together in a cohesive, successful venture. Remember, as Aristotle wisely said, *"Knowing yourself is the beginning of all wisdom."*

1.5
Cultivating Beliefs

"Believe you can, and you're halfway there."
- Theodore Roosevelt

Once you understand how to harness your unique strengths, the next step in your transformation is to cultivate a powerful belief system. Just as you've learned to recognize and leverage your innate talents, it's equally crucial to foster a mindset that truly believes in your capabilities. Theodore Roosevelt's words, quoted above, resonate profoundly within me. This sentiment underscores the transformative power of belief.

While strengths and skills form the foundation of your entrepreneurial journey, it's your beliefs that fuel your drive and determination.

Making Affirmations

To help you on this journey, I'd like to share with you the affirmations I recite daily. These affirmations have anchored my mindset in positivity, resilience, and determination. Consider these affirmations as tools to reinforce your self-worth, amplify your capabilities, and remind yourself of the potential within.

The affirmations:

- *"I can achieve greatness in all areas of my life."*

- *"I possess unique strengths and talents that set me apart."*

- *"I am resilient and bounce back stronger from every challenge I face."*

- *"I embrace failure as an opportunity for growth and learning."*

- *"I can create my own success and shape my destiny."*

- *"I deserve abundance and prosperity in all aspects of my life."*

- *"I am confident in my abilities and trust my decisions."*

- *"I attract positive opportunities and surround myself with supportive individuals."*

- *"I am a magnet for success and attract opportunities that align with my goals."*

- *"I am focused and determined and persist until I achieve my desired outcomes."*

- *"I can overcome any obstacle that stands in my way."*

- *"I embrace change and adapt easily to new circumstances."*

- *"I radiate positivity and inspire those around me with my optimism."*

- *"I am a continuous learner, always seeking new knowledge and growth."*

- *"I am guided by my passions, and I pursue my goals with unwavering enthusiasm."*

- *"I am worthy of love, respect, and recognition for my achievements."*

- *"I trust in the process of life, knowing that everything unfolds perfectly for my highest good."*

- *"I let go of self-limiting beliefs and replace them with empowering thoughts."*

- *"I am a leader and positively influence those around me with my actions and words."*

- *"I live in alignment with my values and create a life of authenticity and fulfillment."*

Entrepreneurship is a complex journey, often intertwined with moments of self-doubt and indecision. From my experiences, I've realized the immense power of belief. It's this belief that transforms doubts into opportunities. More than just a static trait, belief is a skill—one that can be nurtured, refined, and strengthened with deliberate effort, unwavering devotion, and a positive mindset.

Central to this transformation is the practice of positive affirmations. These affirmations, when recited with genuine intent and faith, can reshape the very fabric of your mindset, erasing self-imposed limitations and painting a vision filled with endless possibilities. Embrace these affirmations, and let them guide you toward a stronger, more resilient belief in yourself.

1.6

Focusing on Passion

"Passion is energy. Feel the power that comes from focusing on what excites you."
- Oprah Winfrey

Finally, we reach the last section of Part I. By this point, you have equipped yourself with a robust foundation. You understand how to master your mindset and use your strengths to your advantage to succeed on your journey to becoming a BOSS. Next, we will delve deeper into passion.

Passion, as Oprah Winfrey says, is energy. And this energy is the catalyst that propels you forward, turning dreams into reality. It's time to align yourself with the passions that truly ignite your spirit and discover how to infuse this energy into every facet of your entrepreneurial journey.

Discovering Your Passion

Everyone has moments, memories, or experiences that have left a profound mark on their lives. For me, introspection led to the realization that my passions weren't just hobbies but the keys to my authentic self. I recalled the exhilaration of brainstorming innovative ideas, the thrill of crafting compelling narratives, and the satisfaction derived from networking with people through engaging conversations. Upon closer inspection, the puzzle pieces began to fall into place, revealing a landscape of talents I had perhaps disregarded.

The Spark of Alignment

A conversation with a friend once highlighted my natural ability to communicate and connect. This insight was a revelation, illuminating my passion for storytelling and communication. It became evident that this passion was deeply connected to my entrepreneurial aspirations. Recognizing this alignment, I discerned that my true strength, or Zone of Genius, lay in sales and marketing.

Channeling Passion into Action

With this clarity, every entrepreneurial pursuit became an opportunity to manifest my passion. It felt as if a dormant fire had roared to life, guiding each step with renewed vigor. This alignment of passion and expertise not only invigorated my professional journey but also diminished fears and apprehensions. Challenges transformed into steppingstones; each one leading closer to mastery.

Embracing Your Zone of Genius

Your journey, like mine, will reveal that within you lies a unique blend of gifts and talents. This sweet spot–or Zone of Genius–is where your true self and entrepreneurial spirit converge. It is a transformative realization that can amplify both your personal and professional life.

Understanding and embracing your passion is paramount to entrepreneurial success. Therefore, I invite you to use your newfound knowledge to find your Zone of Genius and let your passion fuel you. When passion is at the heart of your endeavors, even the most ordinary tasks can become extraordinary milestones on your path to success.

Key Takeaways

- Recognize the internal pull toward entrepreneurship and understand that challenges can be viewed as opportunities for growth.

- Employ mind-hacking techniques to overcome limiting beliefs and foster a growth mindset.

- Align your passion with your purpose. Understand that success is something you craft, not something that's predetermined.

- Find where your innate talents and passions converge and let this Zone of Genius guide your endeavors.

- Identify and optimize your unique strengths and talents through introspection.

- Foster a belief system that fuels your drive, determination, and resilience.

- Reinforce your self-worth and amplify your capabilities with positive affirmations.

- Commit to deep introspection to reveal passions that can serve as a guiding light in your entrepreneurial journey.

- Ensure your business strategies align with your passions, transforming even the most ordinary tasks into extraordinary milestones.

- Harness the transformative power of passion to turn your dreams into tangible realities.

Part II:

Strategies

Next, we will explore the strategic and adaptive facets that are essential to truly becoming a BOSS. When you start a business, you need successful **strategies** to ensure that you can sustain and grow it.

Therefore, in Part II, you will:

1) **Master the Art of Preparation:** Grasp the importance of strategic planning, from setting clear goals to breaking them down into actionable tasks, and the role of prioritization in achieving these goals.

2) **Embrace Adaptability:** Learn the significance of flexibility in the entre-preneurial landscape, understanding when and how to pivot strategies based on changing circumstances.

3) **Harness Resilience:** Understand the power of resilience in facing challenges and how adversity can serve as a catalyst for growth and transformation.

4) **Cultivate a Support System:** Recognize the value of building a robust support network, including the roles

of mentors, collaboration, and reciprocal support in enhancing the entrepreneurial journey.

5) **Foster Creativity:** Grasp the strategies to nurture a creative ecosystem, from creating an inspiring workspace to embracing experimentation and valuing diverse perspectives.

2.1
Taking the Leap

"What lies behind us and what lies before us are tiny matters compared to what lies within us."
– Ralph Waldo Emerson

Transitioning to entrepreneurship is more than just a career change; it's a mindset evolution. While it's natural to feel fear and uncertainty, remember that true growth often lies just outside your comfort zone. With every decision, prioritize courage over complacency, knowing that the most significant achievements often come from facing challenges head-on.

Embracing entrepreneurship and becoming a BOSS opens up a world of endless possibilities. By letting go of self-imposed limitations, you'll find the freedom to shape your future. On my journey, I discovered the thrill of taking my fate into my own hands. Defining ourselves by our job titles and familiar routines is quite convenient, but I soon realized that my potential transcended far beyond those boundaries, just as yours does.

Below are three crucial steps you must take when first taking the leap:

1) **Creating a Side Hustle to Experiment and Gain Traction:** Before fully committing to entrepreneurship, consider creating a side hustle while still employed. This is what I did. This approach isn't just about supplementing your income. It offers a platform to test your business idea, gauge market reactions, and adjust accordingly. This safety net can help mitigate the financial risks of venturing into unknown territories.

2) **Determining Financial Needs for Starting the Venture:** Before leaving your steady paycheck behind, it's crucial to understand the financial impli-

cations of your new venture. This involves calculating startup costs, initial investments, and ongoing operational expenses. This financial groundwork will help you understand the capital required and instill the fiscal discipline vital for entrepreneurial success.

3) **Planning a Gradual Transition from Employee to Entrepreneur:** A sudden leap can be overwhelming. Consider a phased approach, gradually reducing your commitments as an employee while increasing your entrepreneurial activities. Part-time roles or freelance projects can help bridge any income gaps, ensuring stability during the early stages of the transition period. Always have a contingency plan to navigate unforeseen challenges.

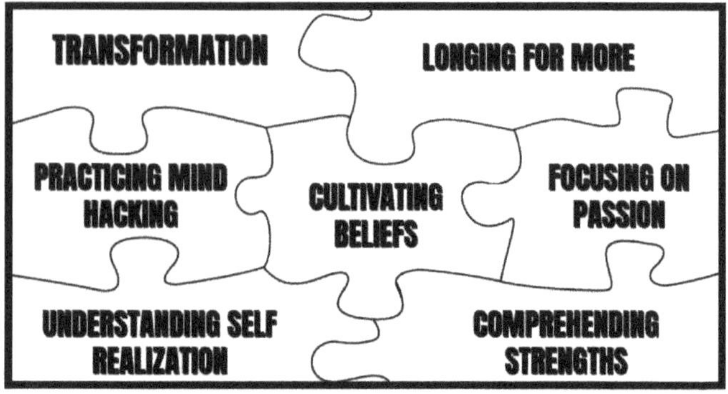

Transitioning from an employee to an entrepreneur is a monumental step that demands careful planning, courage, and a willingness to embrace uncertainty. Once you've decided to take the leap and have begun laying the groundwork, strategic preparation is an essential next step.

2.2

Embracing Strategic Planning

"A goal without a plan is just a wish."
– Antoine de Saint-Exupéry

I sat at my desk, surrounded by a sea of papers and scattered notes. I knew I needed a clear plan and a roadmap to guide me if I wanted to turn my entrepreneurial dreams into reality. Every entrepreneur, at some point, finds themselves surrounded by ideas, aspirations, and the overwhelming need for a clear plan.

Starting an entrepreneurial journey without a clear plan is like setting sail without a compass. Therefore, we will now discuss the art of planning, offering insights into effective techniques and the significance of setting clear goals even in the face of challenges and setbacks.

The Foundation of Goals

Every successful venture begins with a clear set of goals. These goals not only provide direction but also infuse your journey with purpose. Drawing from my experience, I learned that aligning goals with your vision and values is crucial. For instance, one of my initial goals was to establish a strong online presence and build a community of like-minded individuals who resonate with my entrepreneurial journey. This wasn't just a business strategy; it stemmed from a genuine passion for connecting with others and sharing valuable insights. As you set your goals, think about what drives you and how you can translate them into actionable steps.

The Art of Strategic Planning

Setting goals is just the starting point. To bring them to fruition, you need a comprehensive plan. This involves breaking down overarching goals into smaller, actionable tasks. In my case, I created a roadmap that led me to success. I outlined specific tasks such as creating a content calendar, designing engaging graphics, and collaborating with influencers in my niche to establish an online presence. Later, these tasks became a building block in my strategic plan, contributing to the larger objective of building a vibrant online community.

As you create your own tasks, ensure that each one contributes to your larger objective, creating a roadmap to success.

The Power of Prioritization

After gaining experience with strategic planning, I recognized the significance of prioritization. I discovered that not all tasks hold the same level of urgency. It's essential to discern which actions will have the most significant impact on your goals. By prioritizing effectively, you can allocate resources where they matter most.

In my own work, I realized that engaging with my audience through interactive webinars and live Q&A sessions was a high-priority task. These activities allowed me to connect directly with my audience, answer their questions, and provide value in real-time. Thus, I could allocate my time strategically and ensure maximum engagement by focusing on those high-impact activities.

Embracing Flexibility and Growth

The entrepreneurial landscape is constantly evolving. So, while planning is crucial, so is adaptability. There will be times when you'll need to pivot based on market trends or feedback. For example, I once shifted my product launch strategy in response to emerging market demands. Being flexible doesn't mean abandoning your plan but refining it to better suit the changing environment.

The Reward of Clarity and Purpose

Strategic planning delivers a renewed sense of clarity and purpose. By knowing precisely what steps to take each day, you can navigate your path with confidence. Embracing tools and techniques, like time blocking and task prioritization, can further maximize your productivity.

Strategic planning is not just a task but a cornerstone of entrepreneurial success. While my journey underscores the importance of a well-thought-out plan, remember that every entrepreneur's path is unique. As you forge ahead, let this section serve as a guide, reminding you of the power of planning, adaptability, and clear vision. Embrace the art of planning in your journey, and you'll be better equipped to turn your dreams into reality.

2.3
Navigating Challenges

"The human spirit is stronger than anything that can happen to it."
- C.C. Scott.

Every entrepreneur's journey, much like yours, is filled with unexpected challenges and detours. While it's tempting to view these obstacles as setbacks, they can also be opportunities for growth and transformation. This section aims to guide you in building resilience, finding balance amid personal and professional commitments, and harnessing the power of self-care.

Resilience in Adversity

During my journey from employee to entrepreneur, I discovered that adversity was not an impediment but an invitation to rise. Challenges often arise when least expected, testing our determination and resolve. From experience, I learned that these moments of adversity can be catalysts for growth, pushing us to recalibrate, reevaluate, and emerge stronger. As you navigate your entrepreneurial path, remember that setbacks are not signals to retreat but opportunities to rise even higher.

Balancing Personal and Professional Commitments

Navigating the balance between entrepreneurial aspirations and personal commitments is a challenge many face, me included. As an entrepreneur, I've learned that success isn't always a straight path but requires flexibility and adaptability. Balancing the demands of my professional dream while nurturing the relationships that anchored me was an art I had to master.

One of the most profound examples of maintaining this delicate balance was when my wife was diagnosed with cancer. This was shocking news that shook us to the core. During such testing times, I could have allowed angst and uncertainty to overshadow my entrepreneurial pursuits. However, I chose to embrace resilience.

While supporting my wife's recovery from this lethal disease, which included a double mastectomy, I learned the art of compartmentalization. I devoted specific hours to my business, where I worked with unwavering focus. Simultaneously, I was available to support my wife through thick and thin by attending her medical appointments. I supported her during her recovery and offered her the emotional space she required. It was not about putting one aspect of my life on hold for the other; it was about seeking a harmonious rhythm that allowed both aspects to coexist.

Importance of Self-Care

In the midst of challenges, self-care is not just a luxury but a necessity. It's the anchor that keeps us grounded during turbulent times. Whether it's through meditation, journaling, or physical activities, prioritizing self-care ensures you remain resilient and focused, both as an entrepreneur and as an individual. For me, prioritizing self-care meant that I could be a supportive partner to my ailing wife, a devoted entrepreneur, and a resilient individual. I harnessed the power to endure the storm and emerged with clarity and strength.

Weathering the Storms

Challenges, as daunting as they may seem, are opportunities for growth and transformation. My experiences, particularly supporting my wife through her recovery, taught me the true depth of our resilience and the strength of our bond. As you journey through your entrepreneurial endeavors, remember that success lies not in avoiding challenges but in navigating them with grace and determination. Embrace adversity as a chapter that adds depth to your story, propelling you forward in your entrepreneurial journey.

2.4
Building A Support Network

"If you want to go fast, go alone. If you want to go far, go together."
- African Proverb

Every entrepreneur's journey, while unique, benefits immensely from robust support networking. Therefore, this section will discuss the importance of surrounding yourself with mentors, peers, and like-minded individuals who can provide guidance, insights, and camaraderie. While my journey from a Process Improvement Specialist to a visionary BOSS has its personal anecdotes, the broader message is universal: success is often a collective endeavor.

There are three vital notes that underscore the essence of cultivating a support network. These notes are given as follows:

1) **Importance of Mentorship:** Mentors, with their wealth of experience, act as invaluable beacons, guiding us through the often-tumultuous waters of entrepreneurship. The guidance of my mentors is at the heart of my transformation. These experienced individuals who have scaled the peaks you aspire to conquer are invaluable. Their insights and advice, forged through years of experience, can help you steer clear of pitfalls and embrace opportunities. As you navigate your entrepreneurial path, consider seeking out mentors who resonate with your vision and can provide the guidance you need.

2) **The Power of Collaboration:** Entrepreneurship thrives on collaboration. Engaging with a community of like-minded individuals can provide fresh perspectives, innovative solutions, and a sense of camaraderie. Re-

member, every entrepreneur brings a unique set of experiences to the table. By pooling these experiences together, we can create a richer, more informed roadmap to success.

3) **Reciprocal Support:** Support is a two-way street. As much as we gain from our network, it's equally vital to give back. By offering guidance, sharing resources, or simply being there for fellow entrepreneurs, we foster a community spirit that's both nurturing and empowering. This mutual support not only enhances individual journeys but strengthens the entrepreneurial ecosystem as a whole. Personally, in cherishing the success of others, I find a profound connection with others and forge mutual bonds that run deeper than our ambitions. This communal ethos shapes not only my journey but the journey of everyone around me.

I stand not as an individual but as a part of a larger narrative woven by mentors, peers, and communities united by their collective pursuit of greatness. With every step I take and the connection I cultivate, I weave my legacy into the fabric of a dynamic support community. While the entrepreneurial journey is deeply personal, it's enriched by the connections we make and the support we both give and receive. As you progress in your endeavors, remember the power of a strong support network. Let the lessons shared here guide you in building your community, ensuring that as you rise, you lift others with you.

2.5
Harnessing Creativity

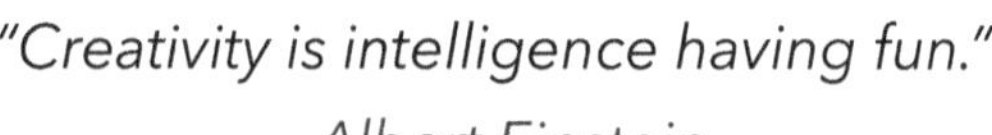

"Creativity is intelligence having fun."
– Albert Einstein

Creativity is not just a distant muse but the driving force that propels our entrepreneurial journey forward. As we navigate the complex world of business, it's essential to recognize that our most transformative ideas often come from a blend of inspiration, experimentation, and collaboration. Therefore, we will now discuss the strategies and practices that can help you cultivate a thriving environment for innovation, ensuring that your entrepreneurial endeavors are not just successful but also uniquely impactful.

Creating a Creative Ecosystem

A conducive environment can be a catalyst for innovation. Below are some strategies for you to consider that are inspired by my own workspace:

1) **Inspiration Wall:** Dedicate a space for images, motivational quotes, and articles that spark your curiosity. This visual collage can serve as a continuous reminder of the world's limitless possibilities.

2) **Incorporating Nature:** Bring potted plants or indoor fountains into your workspace. Such natural touches can offer tranquility and inspire fresh ideas.

3) **Flexible Workspace:** Consider a versatile workspace with movable furniture. Changing your surroundings can rejuvenate your thought process and prevent stagnation.

Embracing Experimentation

Every venture offers opportunities to innovate. With each venture as a laboratory of ideas, you can learn from failures and inch closer to breakthroughs.

1) **Innovative Product Features:** Don't be afraid to experiment with different features for your product. Even if some ideas don't pan out, they'll bring you closer to a market-disrupting concept.

2) **Alternative Marketing Approaches:** Venture beyond traditional marketing strategies. Even if some strategies don't yield immediate results, they can offer valuable insights.

3) **Pilot Projects:** Launch small-scale pilot projects to test unverified concepts without committing significant resources. This approach can provide insights for larger implementations.

Collaborations and Diverse Perspectives

Innovation thrives on diversity. Engaging with individuals from varied backgrounds can offer a wealth of fresh ideas. Here's how:

1) **Cross-Industry Networking:** Attending cross-industry and interdisciplinary

networking events to connect with professionals from outside your immediate circle can offer fresh insights and challenge industry norms.

2) **Mentorship from Unexpected Sources:** Seeking mentorship not just from industry veterans but also from those with unconventional career paths can expand your horizons due to their unique perspectives.

3) **Collaborative Brainstorming Sessions:** Brainstorming with a diverse group of colleagues, professionals, and friends can offer a fusion of varied perspectives that leads to unexpected and innovative solutions.

Creation is not a solitary endeavor but a collective symphony. By fostering the right environment, embracing experimentation, and valuing diverse collaborations, you can unlock unparalleled innovation. Let this section inspire you to harness your creative potential and chart a unique path in your entrepreneurial journey. Remember, every individual adds a unique note to the world's chorus of innovation.

Key Takeaways

Recognize the transition to entrepreneurship as a mindset evolution, where prioritizing courage over complacency can lead to true growth.

- Experiment with a side hustle before fully committing to entrepreneurship. This approach allows you to gauge market reactions and mitigate financial risks.

- Calculate the financial implications of your venture, including startup costs, initial investments, and ongoing operational expenses, to ensure you're adequately prepared.

- Transition from being an employee to an entrepreneur in phases, using part-time roles or freelance projects to bridge any income gaps and ensure stability.

- Break down overarching goals into smaller, actionable tasks, ensuring each contributes to your larger objective and provides a clear roadmap to success.

- Prioritize tasks based on their impact on your goals and allocate resources accordingly to maximize efficiency and outcomes.

- Adapt your strategies based on market trends or feedback, ensuring you remain relevant and effective even in changing landscapes.

- Design a workspace that stimulates innovation, incorporating elements like inspiration spaces, nature, and flexibility to foster creativity.

- Treat each venture as a laboratory of ideas, using failures as steppingstones to inch closer to breakthroughs and success.

- Engage with individuals from various backgrounds to infuse your journey with diverse perspectives, attend cross-industry networking events, and seek mentorship from unconventional sources.

Part III:

Success

Success lies in identifying and honing your top skill into expertise. You will find your purpose at the intersection of your passion and expertise. True success is achieved when you pursue what you're meant for. To excel in business, focus on four key strategies: lead generation, lead conversion, customer ascension, and customer retention. Then, you'll be well on your way to growing your business like a BOSS.

In Part III, you will:

1) Master Strategic Business Scaling: Delve into the principles of scaling a business from a modest monthly revenue to a significantly higher one using strategic moves adaptable to various business contexts.

2) **Optimize Lead Generation:** Harness the importance of lead generation in business expansion and implement techniques to effectively double lead generation efforts, thereby potentially doubling revenue.

3) **Elevate Client Experience:** Implement the strategy of elevating the experience of existing clients through premium value offers, tapping into their needs and desires to generate additional revenue.

4) **Implement Customer Retention Strategies:** Understand and apply the concept of a continuity model in business, where a product is sold once but continues to generate revenue over time, and the impact of introducing complementary products.

5) **Embrace Purpose-Driven Entrepreneurship:** Integrate the transformative power of purpose in business, aligning business goals with values like integrity, compassion, and upliftment for greater success and fulfillment.

3.1
Growing Your Business Like a BOSS

"In business, success is not a coincidence; it's a sequence of strategic moves that unleash the boss within you."
- Myron Golden, Ph. D

In this section, you'll discover the tools to scale your business exponentially to elevate your business like a true BOSS. Get ready to witness how to scale your business from a modest $5,000 per month to a remarkable $54,000 per month using just four strategic moves. These principles are designed to be universally applicable, ensuring you can adapt them to your unique business context.

Imagine you have a core product offer (CPO) priced at $1,000. If you're currently generating $5,000 per month in revenue, that means you're making five sales per month. To achieve these sales, you've likely generated leads. Let's say you're generating 50 leads per month with a 10% conversion rate. That's how you get those five sales. Ready to scale? Let's go.

1) The Power of Lead Generation:

Lead generation is the lifeblood of business expansion. By doubling your leads from 50 to 100 while maintaining your current conversion rate, you can potentially double your revenue.

Picture this: You've established a small consultancy business that offers leadership training. You've been generating 50 leads each month through word of mouth and social media. By introducing lead generation strategies like content marketing, webinars, and strategic partnerships, you manage to double your leads to 100 per month. With the same conversion rate of 10%, you're now closing ten sales per month. This simple enhancement has already doubled your revenue from $5,000 to $10,000 per month.

2) Enhancing Lead Conversion:

Improving your lead conversion process can unlock exponential growth. Techniques like Emotional Cooperation and Logical Justification can help. These strategies focus on creating an environment that encourages buying and providing logical reasons to support that decision. By refining your approach, you can potentially boost conversion rates, leading to a significant increase in revenue. I highly recommend Russel Brunsons' book *Expert Secrets* to learn more.

Using this approach can easily boost conversion rates from 10% to a staggering 20%. Now, not only have you doubled your leads, but you have doubled your conversions as well. Your business revenue just surged to $20,000 per month.

3) Ascend Your Clients:

The third move isn't about leads. It's about customers and clients. It's about taking your existing customer base and elevating their experience through premium value offers.

Let's say you decide to introduce a premium leadership coaching package priced at $5,000. This offering includes personalized one-on-one sessions, customized leadership assessments, and ongoing support. You present this premium value offer (PVO) to your existing clients who have previously purchased your $1,000 leadership training program. With a 10% conversion rate, just two clients decide to take advantage of this enhanced offering, adding an extra $10,000 per month to your revenue.

By tapping into the needs and desires of your existing client base, you can generate additional revenue.

4) Retaining Customers Through Continuity:

Finally, create a continuity model. This is where you sell a product once and continue to earn from it over time. Think SAAS subscriptions or memberships. A particularly potent strategy is forced continuity offers (FCO), where you introduce a mandatory complementary product. Imagine adding a $100 per month SAAS offer to your $1,000 CPO. When you do the math and leverage continuity, the results can be staggering. At twenty sales per month, that's a total of 240 sales at the end of a year. If you multiply those 240 sales by the forced continuity purchase of $100 per month, that's $24,000 per month.

When you add the $24,000 per month from the FCO to the $10,000 per month from the PVO added to the $20,000 per month from the CPO, that's a total of $54,000 per month in four BOSS moves.

When you make your offer, you have to keep in mind that you are not the result, and you don't produce the results for your clients. You sell the outcome, and the process produces the result.

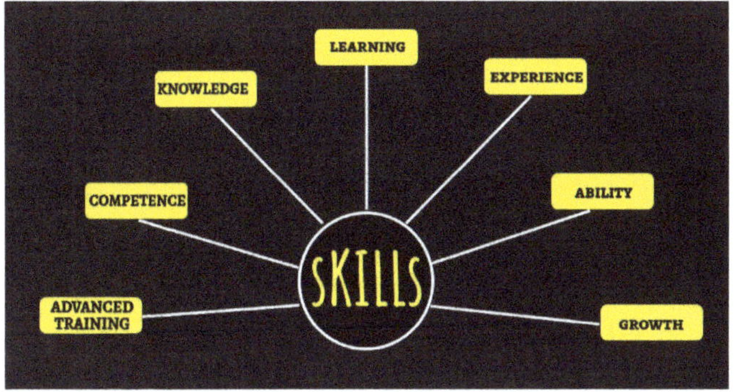

Your journey in business is about more than just numbers; it's about making a meaningful impact. By implementing these four BOSS moves, you're setting the stage for significant growth. Remember, success is a combination of strategic thinking, resilience, and the drive to make a difference. Embrace these principles, and you'll be well on your way to becoming indomitable and achieving success.

3.2

Grasping the Power of Purpose

"Seek ye first the Kingdom of God, and all these things shall be added unto you."
- Matthew 6:33

Eventually, I reached the point in my entrepreneurial journey where I grappled with the essence of true success. Is it solely about wealth and material gains, or is there a deeper, more profound meaning? Was it something that touched the soul and echoed through eternity? This section will guide you through the transformative power of purpose in business, drawing from both ancient wisdom and modern entrepreneurial experiences.

Seeking the Wisdom of Purpose

Guided by my curiosity, I turned to my mentor, and he shared a revelation that would forever redefine my professional life's journey: *"Seek ye first the Kingdom of God."* Quoting the ancient words from Matthew 6:33, he unveiled a philosophy that would breathe life into my pursuit of success.

Defining the Philosophy

The *Kingdom of God within* implies embracing values like integrity, compassion, and a genuine desire to uplift others through your products, services, or contributions. It's about leading with a higher sense of purpose and crafting a business that extends a helping hand to humanity.

Examples of *Seeking the Kingdom Within*

1. **Quality and Empathy:** Ensure your products and services meet market demands and resonate with your customers' needs. Actively seek feedback, listen to their stories, and craft solutions that genuinely improve their lives.

2. **Corporate Social Responsibility:** Recognize the interconnection of society and integrate initiatives that give back to the community. This can range from supporting local charities to adopting environmentally friendly practices.

3. **Empowering Employees:** Foster a culture where your team's growth and contributions are valued. Encourage their talents and create an ecosystem where they feel a sense of purpose and belonging.

Crafting a Legacy of Impact

When your business embraces a purpose-driven approach, it ignites a shared vision that goes beyond profit. It becomes about influencing lives, creating a positive impact, and leaving a legacy that resonates with the philosophy of seeking a higher purpose.

A Legacy of Impact

Your entrepreneurial journey can be a beacon for others. By integrating the philosophy of seeking the *Kingdom of God* within, you can inspire others to align their endeavors with a higher calling. Entrepreneurship can be more than just a business; it can be a force for positive change.

As you move forward, remember that your journey can inspire countless others. By infusing purpose into your business, you can create ventures that symbolize positive societal transformation. It's about intertwining success and impact, ensuring that your entrepreneurial endeavors benefit not just you but the broader community.

Embracing the philosophy of *"Seek ye first the Kingdom of God"* is more than just a concept. It urges you to create a better world for our future generations, ensuring that your business leaves a lasting, positive legacy.

Key Takeaways

- Recognize that success in business arises from a sequence of strategic moves, not mere coincidence.

- Double your leads using tools like content marketing, webinars, and strategic partnerships to potentially double your revenue.

- Implement Emotional Cooperation and Logical Justification to boost conversion rates and foster a buying environment.

- Introduce premium value offers to existing clients to enhance their experience and generate additional revenue.

- Adopt models like SAAS subscriptions or memberships where products sold once continue to generate revenue over time.

- Understand that in business, while you sell the outcome, the process produces the result for your clients.

- Focus on making a meaningful impact and touching lives, going beyond mere profit in your business journey.

- Embrace values like integrity, compassion, and a genuine desire to uplift others in your business endeavors.

- Engage in giving back to the community, be it through supporting charities or adopting eco-friendly practices.

- Align your business goals with the philosophy of *"Seek ye first the Kingdom of God"* to intertwine success with a lasting, positive societal impact.

Part IV:

Impact

Although business is nothing more than solving other people's problems for a profit, you make an **impact** simply by leveraging your entrepreneurial skills to create products, services, and programs that add value to other people's lives.

Finally, in Part IV, you will:

1. **Optimize Personal Growth Strategies:** Discover the interconnectedness of personal growth and societal contribution and how aligning entrepreneurial endeavors with a broader purpose can create lasting positive impacts.

2. **Harness Community Engagement:** Realize the importance of giving back to the community and leveraging entrepreneurial skills to benefit a wider audience, leading to a deeper sense of purpose.

3. **Implement Impactful Initiatives:** Learn how supporting education, offering entrepreneurial mentorship, and initiating community projects can serve as effective methods to make a societal impact.

4. **Refine your Entrepreneurial Journey:** Understand that the path from employee to entrepreneur is a continuous evolution, filled with opportunities to redefine narratives and inspire others.

5. **Embrace Continuous Learning:** Acknowledge that the spirit of entrepreneurship is about ongoing growth, learning, and inspiring others to discover their inner boss.

4.1
Making an Impact

"The best way to find yourself is to lose yourself in the service of others."
– Mahatma Gandhi

By now you'll likely understand that true success transcends far beyond financial gains. As my business flourished and I transformed into an entrepreneur, I discovered the importance of positively influencing others. Therefore, this section explores the link between personal growth and societal contribution and how you can align your entrepreneurial pursuits with a broader purpose, ensuring that your legacy is not just measured in profits but in the positive ripples you create in the world around you.

Discovering the Power of Impact

On my journey, I witnessed my profound influence on others surrounding me. It wasn't just about individual accomplishments anymore; it was about the ripples of positivity I could create in the lives of others. I recognized that my entrepreneurial journey was not a solitary endeavor but a channel through which I could contribute to society, crafting an impactful legacy that transcended my immediate ventures.

It's important that you give back to your community and use your entrepreneurial skills to benefit a broader community. By aligning your business pursuits with your values, you can find a deeper sense of purpose that goes beyond profit. You can align your values with impact in many ways. To give some examples, below is how I did so:

1) **Supporting Education:** Education holds a special place in my heart. Thus, I channeled resources into offering scholarships for underprivileged students. Witnessing their transformation as they pursued their dreams filled my heart with immense satisfaction and fulfillment.

2) **Entrepreneurial Mentorship:** Recognizing the great potential of mentorship, I actively engaged with aspiring entrepreneurs. By sharing my experiences through active supervision, offering guidance, and encouraging their progress and growth, I helped cultivate a new generation of innovators ready to make their mark.

3) **Community Initiatives:** My devotion to the community led me to initiate local projects to uplift underserved individuals. From organizing workshops on financial literacy to collaborating with

nonprofits, these endeavors catalyzed positive transformation and encouraged a sense of unity in my community.

When you give back, you'll see the broader effects of your actions. Small gestures can lead to transformative moments, reinforcing the idea that success is about personal achievements and the positive impact on society.

4.2
Embracing Your Inner BOSS

"Your time is limited, don't waste it living someone else's life. Don't be trapped by dogma, which is living the result of other people's thinking."
– Steve Jobs

With every new day comes a renewed sense of purpose. The restless desire to tap into uncharted potential becomes a driving force. As we reach the final section, you now have a better idea of what it means to be an entrepreneur and how to take your first steps into the unknown. As we approach this final section, let's pause and reflect on the journey we've taken.

Together, we've navigated the intricacies of mind hacking, breaking free from limiting beliefs and fostering a growth-centric mindset. We've discovered the profound synergy of aligning passion with purpose, ensuring every step is a deliberate stride toward crafting your unique success story.

You've been equipped with strategies to transition seamlessly into entrepreneurship, understanding its financial nuances and the significance of phased commitment. We've transformed monumental goals into actionable tasks, emphasizing adaptability, a conducive workspace, and the value of diverse perspectives. In the business realm, you've been shown the blueprint to scale and succeed, understanding that success is a calculated sequence, not mere serendipity. As we conclude, remember that with the insights gained, you're poised to redefine success, intertwining it with purpose, passion, and a lasting positive impact.

To conclude, below are some final tips to help you on your journey.

Embracing Your Inner BOSS

The essence of entrepreneurship lies in recognizing and nurturing your inner BOSS. This transformation requires shedding old beliefs and adopting a mindset of growth, innovation, and endless possibilities. Embracing this new identity means becoming a master of one's own destiny, viewing challenges as opportunities, and aligning actions with passion and purpose.

On my own journey, I become the master of my own mind, hacking into its depths and rewiring its neurons for success. My fear and apprehensions were no longer impediments but challenges to meet head-on. Failure became a steppingstone to greatness. Pursuing passion became my North Star, driving me toward endeavors that align with my purpose and expertise. My Zones of Competence, Excellence, and Genius guided me toward insightful collaborations that amplified my impact.

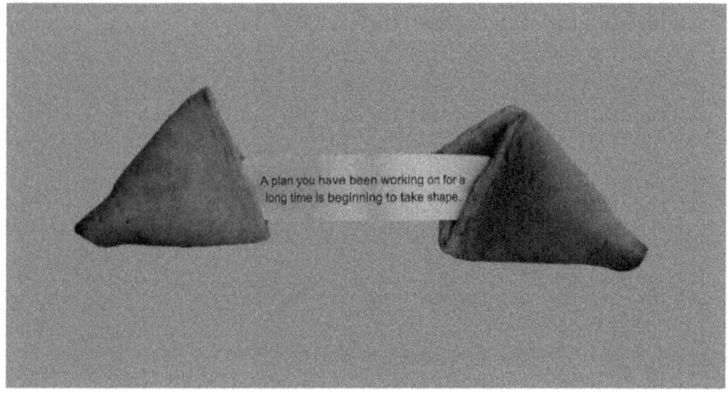

Ensure that you also embrace your inner BOSS and allow yourself to be led by your purpose and expertise. This way, if you refuse to be beaten by failure, you can't lose.

A Call to Empowerment

This book is an invitation for every reader to recognize their potential and embark on their own transformative journey. It's a testament to the nonlinear path to success, filled with unexpected twists and turns. I hope that my own experiences shared here serve as a mirror, reflecting the potential within you.

As this section draws to a close, it's evident that the journey from employee to entrepreneur is a constant evolution that never truly ends. With every step forward, there's an opportunity to redefine your narrative and create a legacy that inspires others. The spirit of entrepreneurship is about continuous growth, learning, and inspiring others to embrace their inner BOSS.

The journey ahead is filled with endless possibilities. With the wisdom of those who've paved the way, like Steve Jobs, offering a renewed sense of purpose and direction. The entrepreneurial spirit is alive and thriving, and the adventure is just beginning.

Key Takeaways

- Recognize that true success goes beyond financial gains, emphasizing the importance of positively influencing others and the broader community.

- Harness the power of your entrepreneurial journey as a means to contribute meaningfully to society, crafting a legacy that extends beyond immediate business ventures.

- Align your business pursuits with deeply held values, leading to a richer sense of purpose. This can manifest in various ways, such as supporting education.

- Appreciate that even small gestures can create transformative moments in others' lives, reinforcing the idea that success is both about personal achievements and the broader societal impact.

- Embrace the mindset shifts required in entrepreneurship, shedding old beliefs and welcoming growth, innovation, and the ability to see challenges as opportunities.

- Overcome fears and apprehensions by viewing failures as steppingstones to success, and let passion be the guiding force in your endeavors.

- Operate within your Zones of Competence, Excellence, and Genius, ensuring you're working from your strengths and areas of expertise to maximize impact.

- Empower yourself and others by understanding that the journey of entrepreneurship is continuous, filled with growth and opportunities to inspire and be inspired.

- Adapt and evolve continuously as you transition from being an employee to an entrepreneur, ensuring your growth, redefinition, and legacy creation are ongoing.

- Draw inspiration from pioneering figures, like Steve Jobs, to provide direction and purpose in your entrepreneurial journey.

Parting Words

"The future belongs to those who believe in the beauty of their dreams."
- Eleanor Roosevelt

Congratulations on completing *Rise2Boss: From Employee to Successfully Unemployed*. As we reflect on the insights shared, remember that these lessons aren't just my experiences but tools for you to kindle your entrepreneurial spirit.

The Power of Mindset: A resilient mindset is essential for transitioning from an employee to an entrepreneur. By challenging self-imposed boundaries and fostering a growth mindset, you can transform apprehensions into opportunities. Embrace this mental evolution as a cornerstone of your success.

Passion and Purpose: Dive deep within to uncover your passions and purpose. Aligning with your skills can be the catalyst for genuine, lasting success. Let passion, when paired with purpose, be your guiding compass.

Impact and Responsibility: Entrepreneurship offers a unique platform to make a difference. It's more than personal achievements; it's about creating positive change. By integrating social responsibility into your ventures, you can inspire others and drive meaningful societal change.

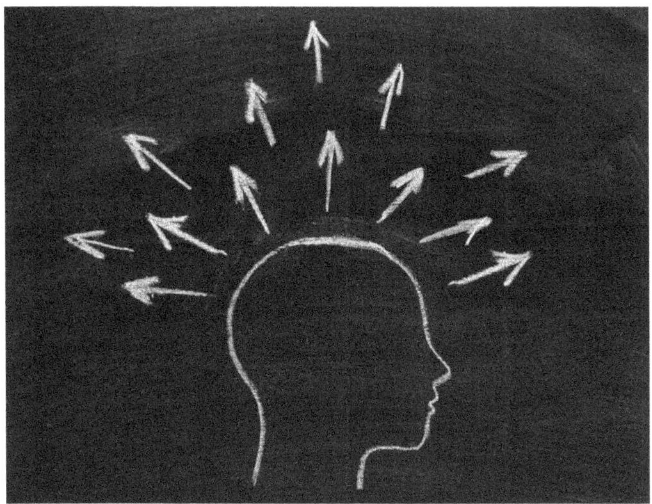

With the insights from this book, you're equipped to navigate the challenges of entrepreneurship. Remember, it's not just about overcoming obstacles but also about making a positive impact on the world around you. This isn't the end but a fresh start. Harness the power of community, adaptability, and innovation. Your potential is vast, and your ability to make a difference is immeasurable.

So, forge your path, understanding that the world needs your unique contributions. Success is an opportunity to uplift and inspire others, leaving a lasting legacy behind. Armed with the wisdom and inspiration garnered from these chapters, you stand on the precipice of a transformative adventure. The world needs your brilliance, your passion, and your unique voice. Join me by booking a call to discuss how you can begin your own journey from employee to entrepreneur in just 120 days.

Click here to book your call →
www.rise2boss.com

I finish this book with these profound lines: *"The future belongs to those who believe in the beauty of their dreams!"*

Acknowledgments

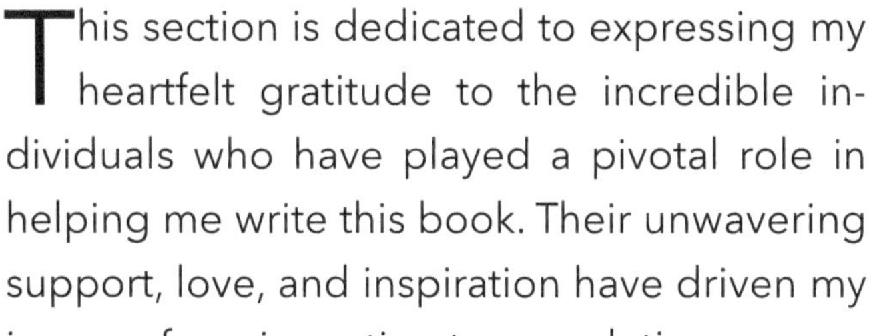

This section is dedicated to expressing my heartfelt gratitude to the incredible individuals who have played a pivotal role in helping me write this book. Their unwavering support, love, and inspiration have driven my journey from inception to completion.

To my beautiful wife, *Talondia Becton*, you have been my ultimate muse and unwavering pillar of strength. Your love, encouragement, and belief in me have fueled my creativity and kept me steadfast on this path. Your resilience and grace in facing challenges have inspired me beyond measure.

To my children, *Aneda, Daisha, Dezmond, George*, and *Trey* (James III), and my cherished grandchildren, *Jamya, Aniyah, Addison*, and *Yara*, you have inadvertently become the wellspring of inspiration that flows through the pages of this book. Your innocent curiosity, boundless energy, and unwavering love have reminded me of the significance of forging a path that empowers future generations.

I extend my heartfelt gratitude to my parents, *Jacquline* and *James Becton Sr.*, for instilling the values of perseverance, diligence, and integrity in me. Your unwavering support and belief in my abilities have been a constant source of motivation throughout my personal and professional life. To my grandparents, *Agnes Morrow*, *Mattie Steele*, and (my only living grandmother-in-love) *Margaret Mosley*, your wisdom and guidance have shaped me into who I am today.

I would also like to acknowledge Bishop *Michael Ingram* and his wife, First Lady *Kimmie Ingram*, for their invaluable guidance, steadfast faith, and unwavering belief in my potential. Your support and encouragement have been instrumental in keeping my spirit ignited. Furthermore, thank you to Pastor's First Assistant, *Tireca Thompson*, who has been one of my biggest cheerleaders, for always supporting me.

To my siblings, *Cedric* (Yolonda) *Whitmore, Octavius Becton, Kirstan Whitmore, Jamarious Becton, Latrisse* (Kevin) *Cassey, Maurico* (Toya) *White, Corey Little*, and *Ladaria* (Anthony) *Boyd*, your unwavering love and support have been a constant source of strength. Your presence has enriched my life in countless ways, and I am grateful for each of you.

To all the friends, family members, and mentors who have supported me throughout this incredible journey, your belief in my vision and steadfast encouragement have inspired me. Your feedback, guidance, and prudence have enriched this book.

To my readers who have embarked on this transformative journey with me, thank you for your assurance and belief in the power of self-discovery and transformation. I hope this book empowers you to unleash your inner BOSS, overcome your apprehensions, and embrace the limitless possibilities within you.

Finally, I am indebted to the countless people whose names I could not mention individually but whose impact on my life is immeasurable. Your influence, support, and inspiration have woven into this book's fabric.

Together, let us forge a path of purpose, passion, and success as we unleash our inner BOSSes and embrace the boundless potential within us all.

With heartfelt gratitude,

James Becton